Karen Frazier
Barbara Hoskins
Ritsuko Nakata
Steve Wilkinson

with
songs and chants by Carolyn Graham

OXFORD
UNIVERSITY PRESS

Icons

Let's Go Student Book 5 consists of eight units, with a review section after every two units. Every unit is divided into six lessons. Each lesson is identified by a colorful icon. The same icons are used for reference on the corresponding pages in both the *Workbook* and the *Teacher's Book*.

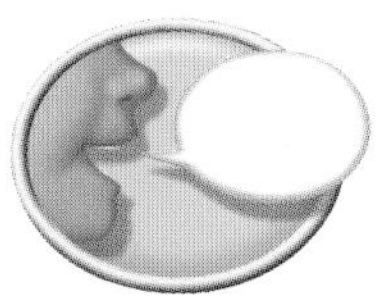

Let's Talk
Functional dialogue

Let's Sing or **Let's Chant**
Interactive song or chant based on the new grammatical structure

Let's Learn
New grammatical structure

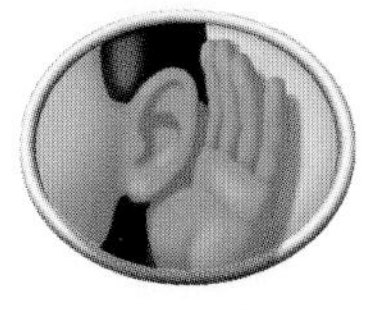

Let's Listen
Listening test and unit review

Let's Read
Reading skills development

Let's Review
Further review after every two units

Table of Contents

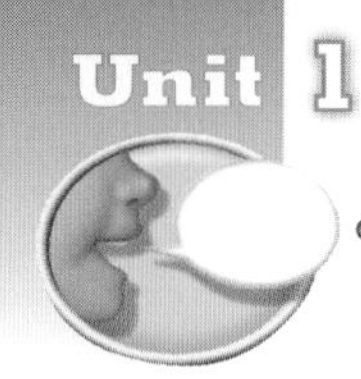

Let's Talk

My name's Mark. I'm 12. I have one sister. She's 6. My best friend is Kevin. I like to play with my pets. I have two dogs and a bird.

Hi! I'm Beth. I'm 10 years old. I don't have any brothers or sisters. My best friend is Anna. I like to play computer games.

I'm	Beth.	My	name's Mark.
	12.		best friend is Anna.
	10 years old.		

Ask and answer.

What's her name?
Her name is Anna.

Does she have any brothers or sisters?
Yes, she has two brothers.

How old is she?
She's 11 years old.

What does she like to do?
She likes to play soccer.

What about you?

What's your name?
How old are you?
Do you have any brothers or sisters?
What do you like to do?
Who's your best friend?

Let's Learn

Mark likes animals very much. He feeds his pets every day. He wants to be a veterinarian.

Anna is a good soccer player. Last Saturday she kicked a goal and won the game. She wants to be a coach.

Kevin likes to draw. He built a model rocket for the science fair. He wants to be an engineer.

Beth likes computers. Sometimes she writes stories on the computer, and sometimes she plays games. She wants to work with computers.

build → built

Ask the questions.

Here's an example.

A: What does she want to be?
B: She wants to be an engineer.

1. A: ______________?
   B: She wants to be an engineer.

2. A: ______________?
   B: She likes to play volleyball.

3. A: ______________?
   B: He's going to play soccer.

4. A: ______________?
   B: She has to clean up her room.

5. A: ______________?
   B: He wants to be a veterinarian.

6. A: ______________?
   B: They're going to go shopping.

7. A: ______________?
   B: He has to wash the dishes.

8. A: ______________?
   B: They like to go camping.

Answer the questions.

1. What did they do yesterday?
2. What does he want to do?
3. Why did she stay home yesterday?
4. Which one is bigger?

Let's Read

Karlie's Report

I love animals! Someday I want to be a veterinarian. Last year I volunteered at the zoo during summer vacation. I learned a lot about taking care of animals.

Every day I helped the zookeepers feed the animals. Some of the animals ate grains and others ate meat. Some of them liked to eat dog food or cat food!

Sometimes we gave the animals treats. First, we put some fruit, like peaches and apples, in water. Then, we froze the water. The animals really liked their frozen fruit treats.

Working at the zoo was fun. I want to do it again next summer.

New Words

someday	grains
volunteered	treats
during	froze
taking care of	frozen
zookeepers	

Answer the questions.

1. What did Karlie do during summer vacation?
2. Do some zoo animals like to eat dog food?
3. Did Karlie and the zookeepers give the animals frozen fish treats?
4. Why does Karlie want to work at the zoo again?

True or false?

1. Karlie wants to be a zookeeper.
2. All of the animals ate meat.
3. Karlie and the zookeepers never gave the animals treats.
4. Karlie wants to be a veterinarian next summer.

Choose a title.

Which is the best title for Karlie's report?

a. Working at a Zoo
b. Going to a Zoo
c. Eating at a Zoo

What about you?

Do you like animals?
Do you like to go to the zoo?

Vocabulary

What does "volunteer" mean?

a. to work
b. to learn
c. to visit

Sounds and Sentences

The snail likes to eat a snack in the snow.

The small boy smeared the paint and smiled.

She Wants to Be an Engineer

She wants to be an engineer.
She wants to be an engineer.
Her mother was an engineer,
Her father was one, too.
She wants to be an engineer.

She doesn't want to be a nurse.
She doesn't want to be a sailor.
She doesn't want to be an English teacher.
She wants to be an engineer.

She wants to be an engineer.
She doesn't want to be a lawyer.
She doesn't want to be a rich man's wife,
Oh, no. She wants to be an engineer,
Just like her mama.
She wants to be an engineer.

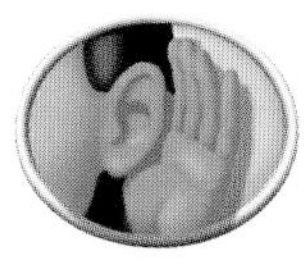

Let's Listen

Listen and number the boxes.

Listen to the answer and check the question.

1. ☐ What did she do yesterday?
   ☐ What is she going to do?

2. ☐ What does he like to do?
   ☐ What does he have to do?

3. ☐ What does she want to be?
   ☐ What does she do?

4. ☐ Who's his best friend?
   ☐ Who's his brother?

Let's Talk

Anna: Hi, Mark!
Mark: Hi, Anna. Where are you going?
Anna: I'm going to visit my cousins. What about you?
Mark: I'm waiting for my aunt.

Anna: What does she look like?
Mark: She has short hair.
Anna: Is that her over there?
Mark: No. My aunt has blond hair and she wears glasses.
Anna: Is that her by the bench?
Mark: Yes, it is. Thanks, Anna.

Mark: Aunt Mary, here I am!

Anna: Oh, my train is leaving. I have to go!
Mark: OK. Have a good trip.
Anna: Thanks. See you Monday.

Have a good trip.
Thanks. See you Monday.

Hair Color	Hair Style	Eye Color
blond hair, red hair	curly hair, straight hair	blue eyes
brown hair		green eyes
gray hair, black hair	long hair, short hair	brown eyes
		black eyes

Ask and answer.

Let's Learn

Anna's train is coming into the station. Her aunt, uncle, and cousins are waiting for her. Her aunt is the woman in the blue and yellow dress. Her uncle is the man with glasses and red hair. Her cousin Maria is the girl with long brown hair. Her cousin Pedro is the boy in the yellow cap.

Grammar Focus

Her uncle is the man	with red hair.
Her aunt is the woman	in the yellow cap.
Her cousin is the girl	
Her cousin is the boy	

Ask and answer.

Which girl is Brian's cousin?

His cousin is the girl | with curly red hair.
| in the blue pants and striped shirt.

Play a game.

Ask questions about the pictures above. Here's an example.

A: I'm thinking of a man.
B: Is he the man with blond hair?
A: No, he isn't.
B: Is he the man with gray hair?
A: Yes, he is.
B: Is he Brian's grandfather?
A: Yes, he is.

Let's Read

Allison's Report

This is a report about two families. One family is small, and one family is big.

This is Diane. She is my cousin. She lives in England. She lives with her father, mother, and sister. They live in an apartment. Diane's grandparents live far away.

This is Roberto. He is my pen pal. He lives in Chile. He lives with his father, mother, brothers, sisters, and grandparents. They live in a big house. His aunt and uncle and cousins live in a house next door.

New Words

England
apartment
far away
Chile
next door

Answer the questions.

1. Does Diane have a big family or a small family?
2. Who does Diane live with?
3. Do Roberto's grandparents live with him?
4. Who lives next door to Roberto?

True or false?

1. Diane lives in an apartment in England.
2. Diane's grandparents don't live with her.
3. Roberto has a small family.
4. Roberto's cousins live far away.

Choose a title.

Which is the best title for Allison's report?

a. Two Kinds of Families
b. Diane's Family
c. Roberto's Family

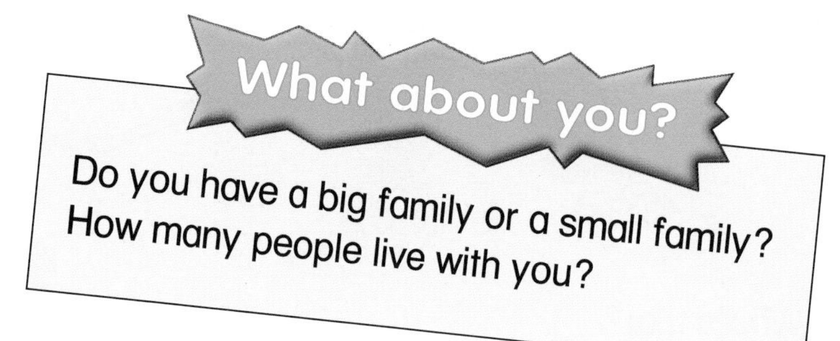

Vocabulary

What does "grandparents" mean?

a. mother and father
b. aunt and uncle
c. grandmother and grandfather

Sounds and Sentences

The swallows swooped down near the swan on the swing.

The twins twirled in the twinkling twilight.

Let's Chant

Who's That Girl?

Who's that?
Who's that?
Who's that girl? Who's that?
Who's that girl in the short black dress?
  That's my older sister, Bess.

Who's that?
Who's that?
Who's that boy? Who's that?
Who's that boy with the baseball bat?
  That's my younger brother, Pat.

Who's that woman in the long red skirt?
Who's that man in the bright green shirt?
Who's that boy with the curly hair?
Who's that girl with the teddy bear?

  That's my mother in the long red skirt.
  That's my father in the bright green shirt.
  That's my brother with the curly hair.
  That's my sister with the teddy bear.

Let's Listen

Listen and circle.

1.

a b

2.

a b

3.

a b

4.

a b

Listen and number the pictures.

Let's Review

A. Fill in the blanks. Then say and act.

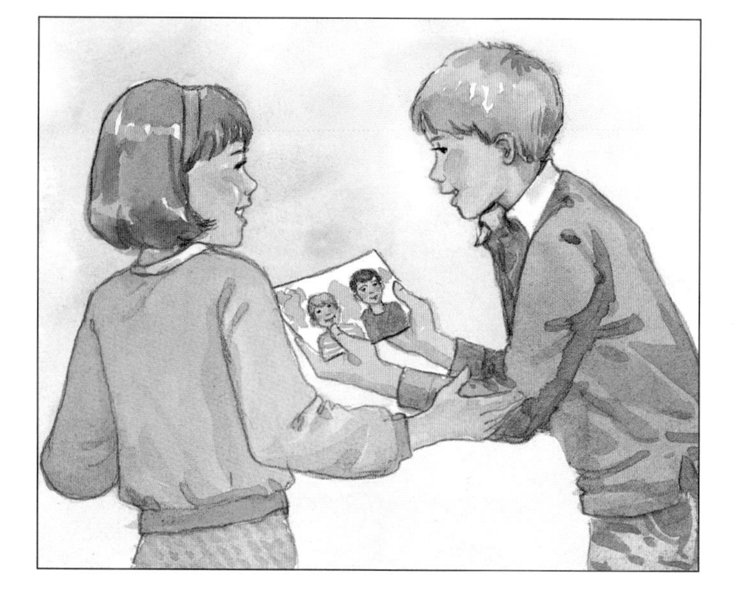

1. **Beth:** What's his name?
   Mark: ____________________ Tom.
   Beth: ______________________?
   Mark: Yes, he has one sister.

2. **Anna:** ______________________?
   Mark: She has short hair.
   Anna: Is that her over there?
   Mark: ___. ______________ blond hair and she ________________.

B. Ask your partner.

What did you do yesterday?
What are you going to do tomorrow?
What do you like to do?
What do you have to do after school?

C. Answer the questions.

What do you look like?
What does your teacher look like?
What does your best friend look like?

D. Listen to the answers. Number the questions.

___ What does he look like?
___ What does she like to do?
___ What is she doing?
___ What is he going to do after school?

E. Listen and number the pictures.

Let's Talk

Beth: Hi, Anna! Where are you going?
Anna: We're going to go camping.
Beth: That sounds like fun!

Anna's mother: Would you like to go camping with us, Beth?
Beth: Sure! I'd love to. I'll go and ask my parents.

Anna: Hello?
Beth: Hi, Anna. This is Beth. Good news! I can go!
Anna: Great!
Beth: What will I need?
Anna: You'll need a sleeping bag and a pillow. Bring some warm clothes, too. It'll be cold at night.
Beth: OK. I'll be at your house in twenty minutes.
Anna: Good. See you soon!

Would you like to go camping with us?
Sure! I'd love to.
Thanks, but I can't.

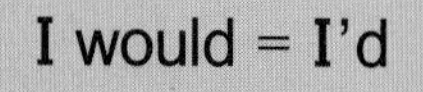

Ask and answer.

He's going to go camping tomorrow.
What will he need?
He'll need a tent and a flashlight.

I will = I'll	She will = She'll
You will = You'll	It will = It'll
He will = He'll	They will = They'll

Say these.

It'll be cold tomorrow.
I'll need a jacket.

It'll be hot tomorrow.
I won't need a jacket.

will not = won't

Let's Learn

Anna's family and Beth are on their way to the campground. The girls are planning their camping trip.

Tomorrow morning they'll go hiking. In the afternoon they'll go canoeing.

On Sunday morning they'll go fishing and then they'll go swimming.

Every night they'll have a campfire. It'll be fun!

Ask and answer.

What will they do tomorrow?
They'll go canoeing.

Yes or no?

Ask questions about the pictures above.

Will they need a canoe? Yes, they will.
No, they won't.

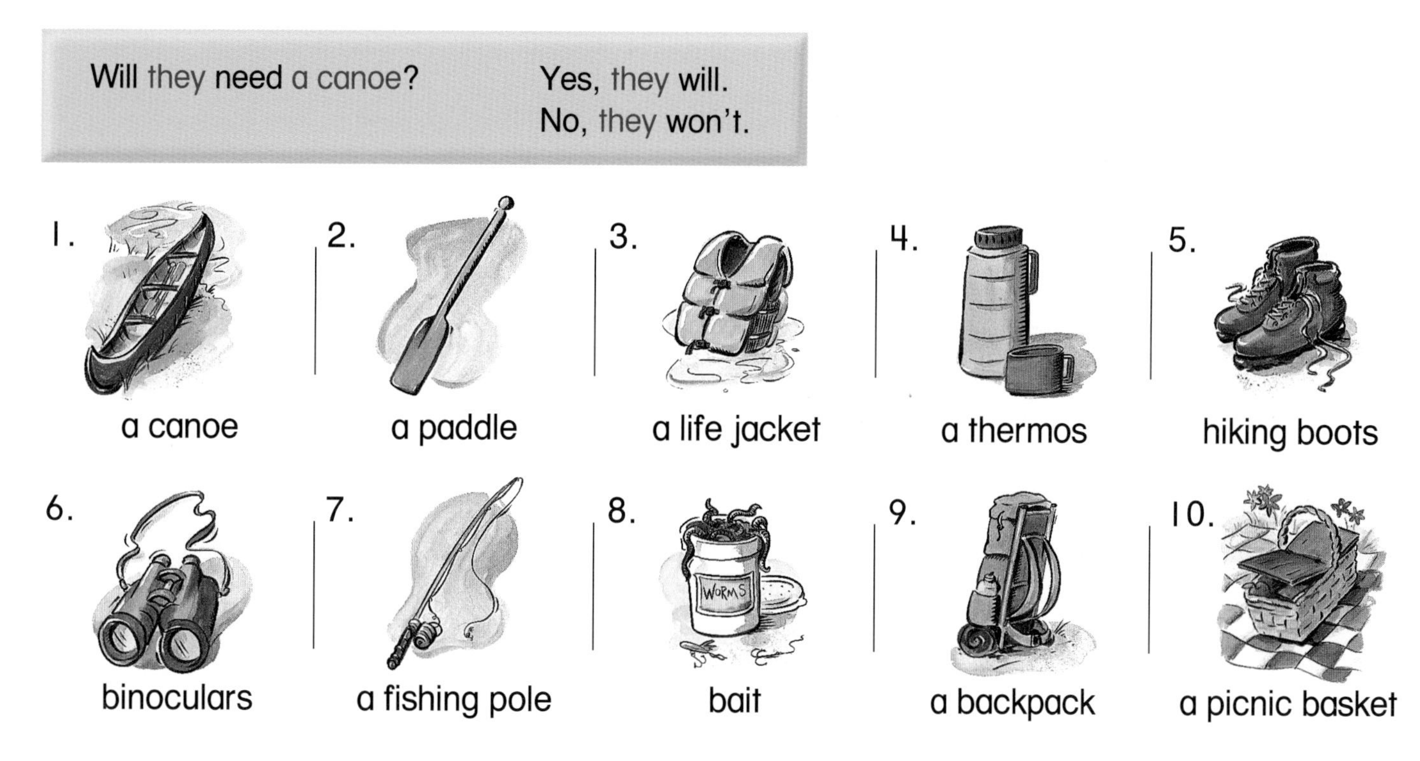

Steve's Report

I like collecting leaves. They have many different shapes. You can make a lot of things with leaves. One fun project is leaf pictures.

This is how to make a leaf picture. You will need leaves, paper, paint, a paintbrush, and glue. First, glue the leaves onto the paper. Wait for an hour. Then, paint over the leaves and the paper. Let the paint dry. Then, carefully take the leaves off the paper. You will see a beautiful leaf pattern.

You can make birthday cards, wrapping paper, or other things with your leaf pictures. Have fun!

New Words

different	wait
shapes	hour
project	pattern
paintbrush	birthday cards
onto	wrapping paper

Answer the questions.

1. Do all leaves have the same shape?
2. What do you need to make leaf pictures?
3. What do you do first?
4. What can you make with leaf pictures?

Put the steps in order.

_____ Paint over the leaves and the paper.
_____ Take the leaves off the paper.
_____ Glue the leaves onto some paper.

Choose a title.

Which is the best title for Steve's report?

a. Making a Birthday Card
b. Collecting Leaves
c. Leaf Pictures

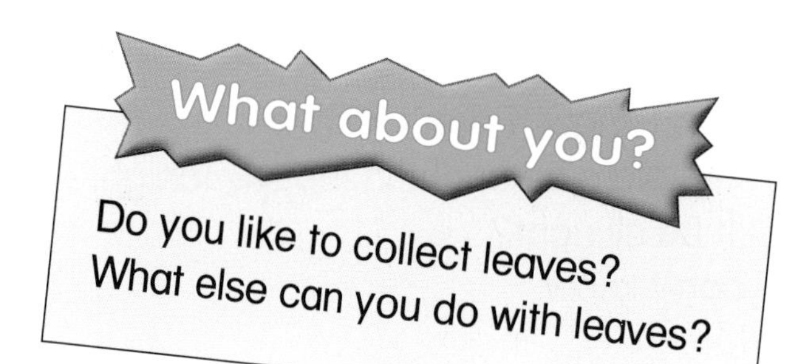

Vocabulary

What does "different" mean?

a. the same
b. not the same
c. beautiful

Sounds and Sentences

Let's Sing

The Weatherman Song

Weatherman, weatherman, listen to me.
How will the weather be?
How will the weather be?
Weatherman, weatherman, listen to me.
How will the weather be tomorrow?

Will it rain?
No, no.
Will it snow?
No, no.
Will the sun come out?
I don't know. I don't know.
Will the stars be bright in the sky tonight?
Will it be all right?
I don't know.

Weatherman, answer me, yes or no?
Will it rain tomorrow? Will it snow?
Answer me, weatherman, yes or no?
Will it rain tomorrow? Will it snow?

Will it rain?
No, no.
Will it snow?
No, no.
Will the moon come out?
I don't know. I don't know.
Will the stars be bright in the sky tonight?
Will it be all right?
I don't know.

Let's Listen

Listen and check.

Listen and check.

							BAIT	
1. Miku								
2. Mario								
3. Lindsay								
4. Kent								

Let's Talk

Mark: I'm worried about the math test tomorrow. Math is so hard.
Beth: No, it isn't. It's easy.
Mark: Not for me. I don't like numbers.

Beth: I think geography is harder than math.
Mark: No, it isn't. Geography is easier. It's about real places. It's more fun!
Beth: No, it's not!

Mark: Hey, Kevin. What do you think?
Kevin: Well, I think geography is easy.
Mark: I think so, too.
Kevin: But math is easy, too. They're both easy!

What do you think?
I think geography is easy.

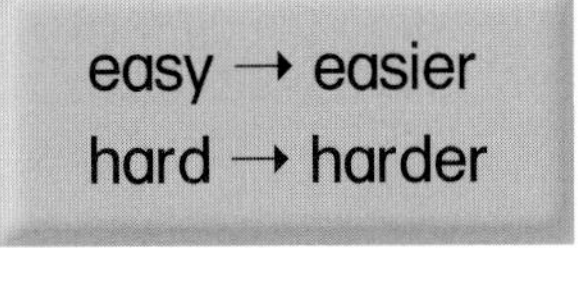

Say these.

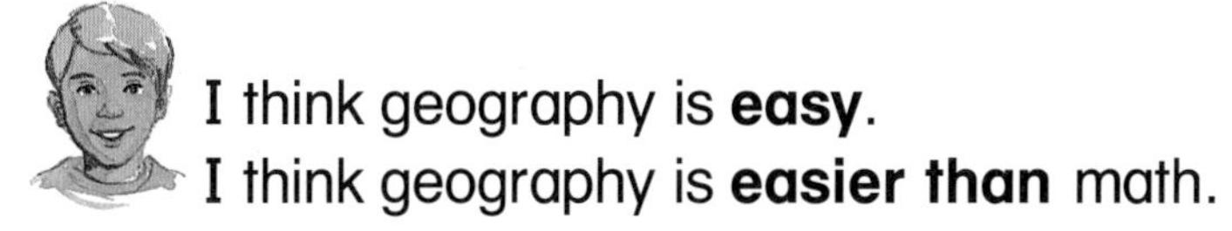

I think geography is **easy**.
I think geography is **easier than** math.

I think math is **hard**.
I think math is **harder than** geography.

Play a game.

Toss two coins onto the game board. Make a sentence.

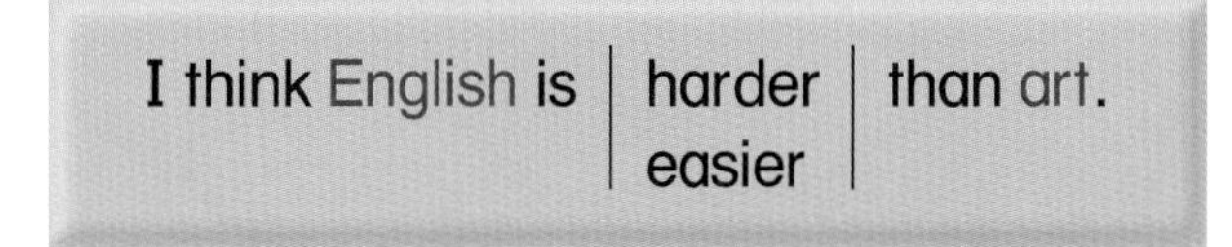

Ask your partner.

Which subject is easier, __________ or __________?
Which subject is harder, __________ or __________?
What's your favorite subject?

Let's Learn

Mark had to make a report about animals for his science class. He went to the library and got some good books.

Mark read about the speeds and sizes of many different animals. He took a lot of notes.

He compared the speeds of several animals. He was surprised. The jackrabbit is as fast as the racehorse and it is faster than the greyhound. The cheetah is the fastest animal on land.

At home, Mark looked at his notes again. Then he made a poster for his report.

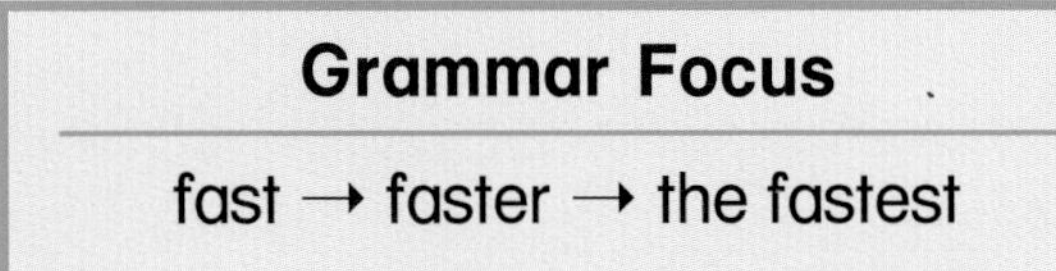

Grammar Focus

fast → faster → the fastest

Ask and answer. Compare the animals.

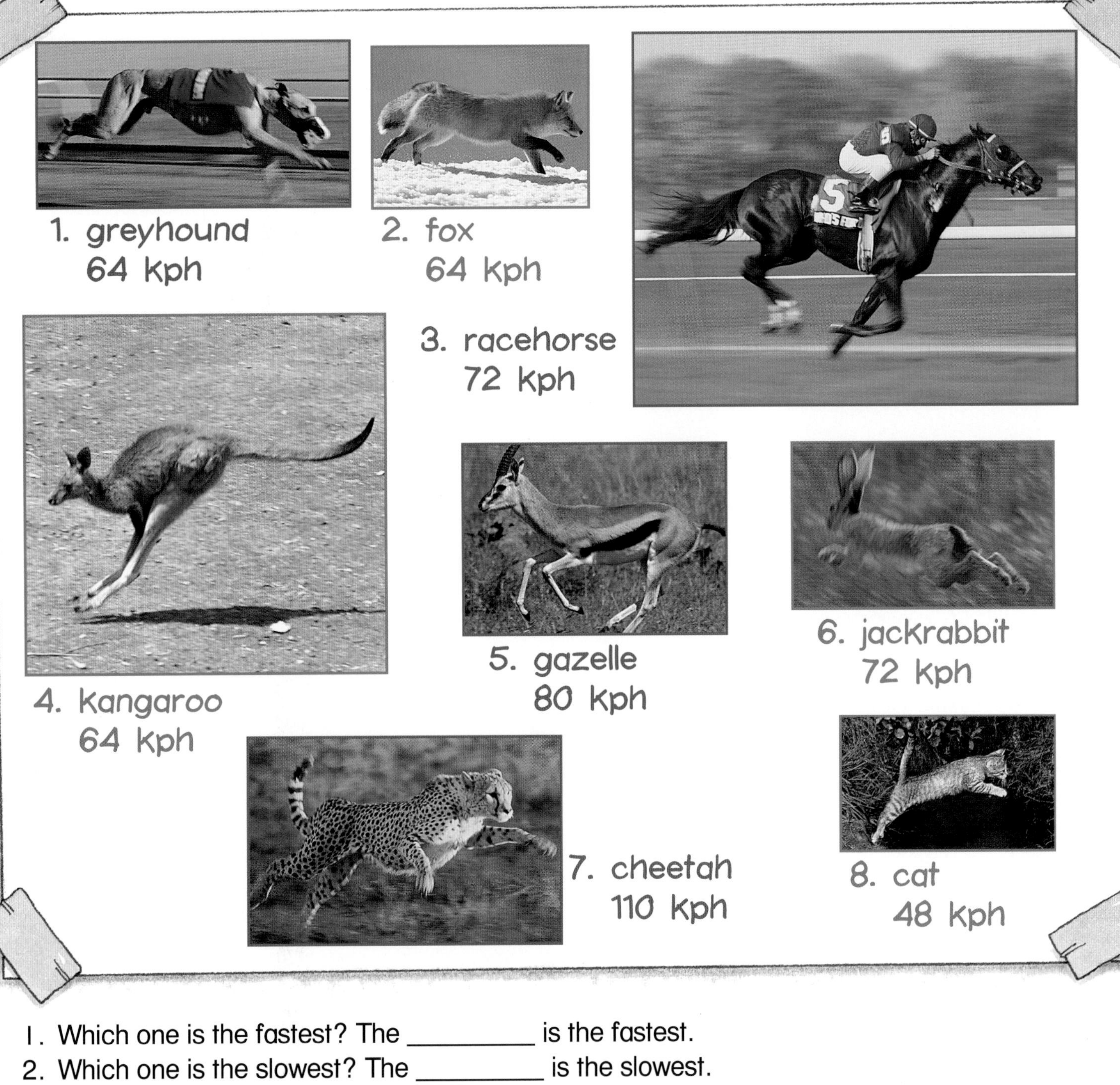

1. Which one is the fastest? The __________ is the fastest.
2. Which one is the slowest? The __________ is the slowest.
3. Which one is the biggest? The __________ is the biggest.
4. Which one is the smallest? The __________ is the smallest.

Make sentences about the poster above.

1. Use *bigger, smaller, slower,* or *faster.*
   The racehorse is bigger than the jackrabbit.
2. Use *as fast as.*
   The fox is as fast as the kangaroo.

Let's Read

Rick's Report

Dinosaurs lived millions of years ago. Some dinosaurs were very big and some were very small.

The smallest dinosaur was the Compsognathus. It was smaller than a chicken. It had feathers, too. The Compsognathus ate small animals.

The biggest dinosaur was the Brachiosaurus. It was taller than all the other dinosaurs. The Brachiosaurus ate leaves and plants.

The Tyrannosaurus Rex was not as big as the Brachiosaurus, but it was very fierce. It liked to fight other dinosaurs. It ate smaller dinosaurs and other animals.

There are no dinosaurs today, but you can see dinosaur bones in a museum.

New Words

dinosaurs	plants
millions of years ago	Tyrannosaurus Rex
very	fierce
Compsognathus	fight
feathers	bones
Brachiosaurus	

Answer the questions.

1. When did dinosaurs live?
2. Was the Compsognathus as big as a chicken?
3. What did the Tyrannosaurus Rex eat?
4. Which dinosaur was the biggest?

True or false?

1. The Compsognathus was the smallest dinosaur.
2. The Brachiosaurus had feathers.
3. Today dinosaurs live in zoos.
4. You can see dinosaur bones in a museum.

Choose a title.

Which is the best title for Rick's report?

a. Dinosaurs
b. The Brachiosaurus and The Compsognathus
c. Museums

Vocabulary

What does "fierce" mean?

a. likes to eat leaves and plants
b. likes to eat smaller dinosaurs
c. likes to fight

Sounds and Sentences

The stagecoach was faster than the stork in the storm.

Andy ate strawberries in a stroller by the stream.

Let's Sing

An Elephant Is Bigger Than a Flea

An elephant is bigger than a flea.
I said an elephant is bigger than a flea.
An elephant is stronger.
An elephant lives longer.
An elephant is bigger than a flea.

An elephant is better than a flea.
Why?
Because an elephant is easier to see in the dark.
An elephant is bigger, much, much bigger.
An elephant is bigger than a flea.

A crocodile is bigger than a fly.
I said a crocodile is bigger than a fly.
A crocodile is stronger.
A crocodile lives longer.
A crocodile is bigger than a fly.

A crocodile is better than a fly.
Why?
Because a crocodile can smile and he can cry.
A crocodile is better.
He can even knit a sweater.
A crocodile is better than a fly.

Let's Listen

Listen and check the answer.

1. ☐ He thinks science is harder than literature.
   ☐ He thinks science is easier than literature.

2. ☐ She thinks history is harder than music.
   ☐ She thinks history is easier than music.

3. ☐ He thinks math is harder than geography.
   ☐ He thinks geography is harder than math.

4. ☐ She thinks English is easier than art.
   ☐ She thinks art is easier than English.

Listen. Which words do you hear? Circle the words.

1.	2.	3.	4.
history	art	physical education	math
geography	literature	English	science
music	science	music	history
English	math	art	literature

Listen and circle the word.

1.

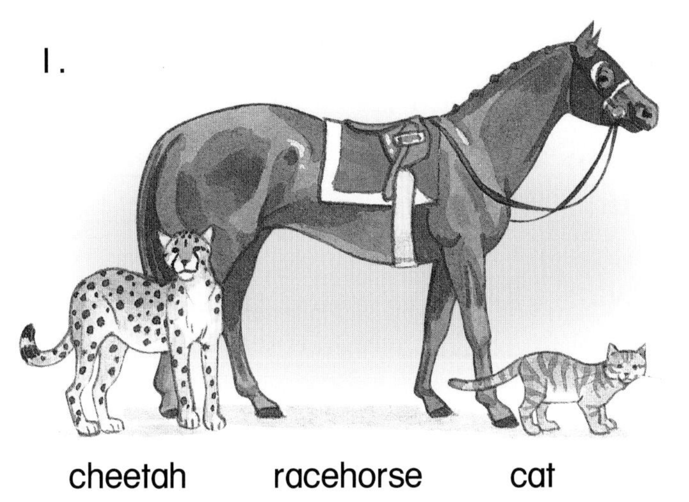

cheetah racehorse cat

2.

kangaroo fox gazelle

3.

jackrabbit	fox	cheetah
72 kph	64 kph	110 kph

4.

jackrabbit	greyhound	cat
72 kph	64 kph	48 kph

Let's Review

A. Fill in the blanks. Then say and act.

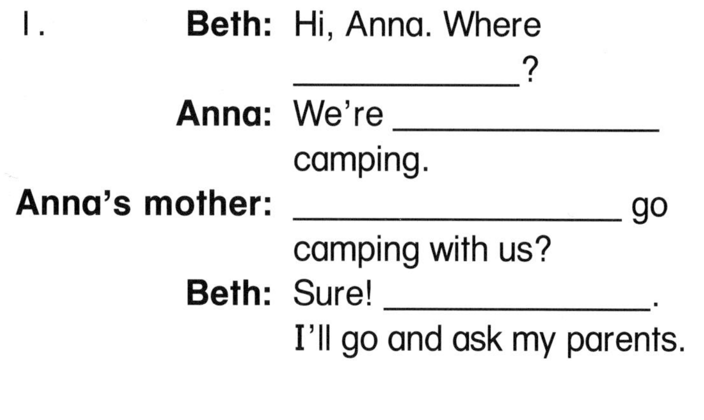

1. **Beth:** Hi, Anna. Where ____________?
Anna: We're ______________ camping.
Anna's mother: _________________ go camping with us?
Beth: Sure! ______________. I'll go and ask my parents.

2. **Mark:** ___________ easier, geography or math?
Beth: Well, I think _______________.
Mark: Hey Kevin, _______________ think?
Kevin: I think _____________, but ________, too. They're both easy!

B. Ask your partner. Circle the answer.

What do you think? Is English easy or hard?

English	easy	hard
math	easy	hard
geography	easy	hard
art	easy	hard

literature	easy	hard
history	easy	hard
music	easy	hard
science	easy	hard

C. Answer the question.

What are you going to do this weekend?

D. Listen to the questions. Circle the answers.

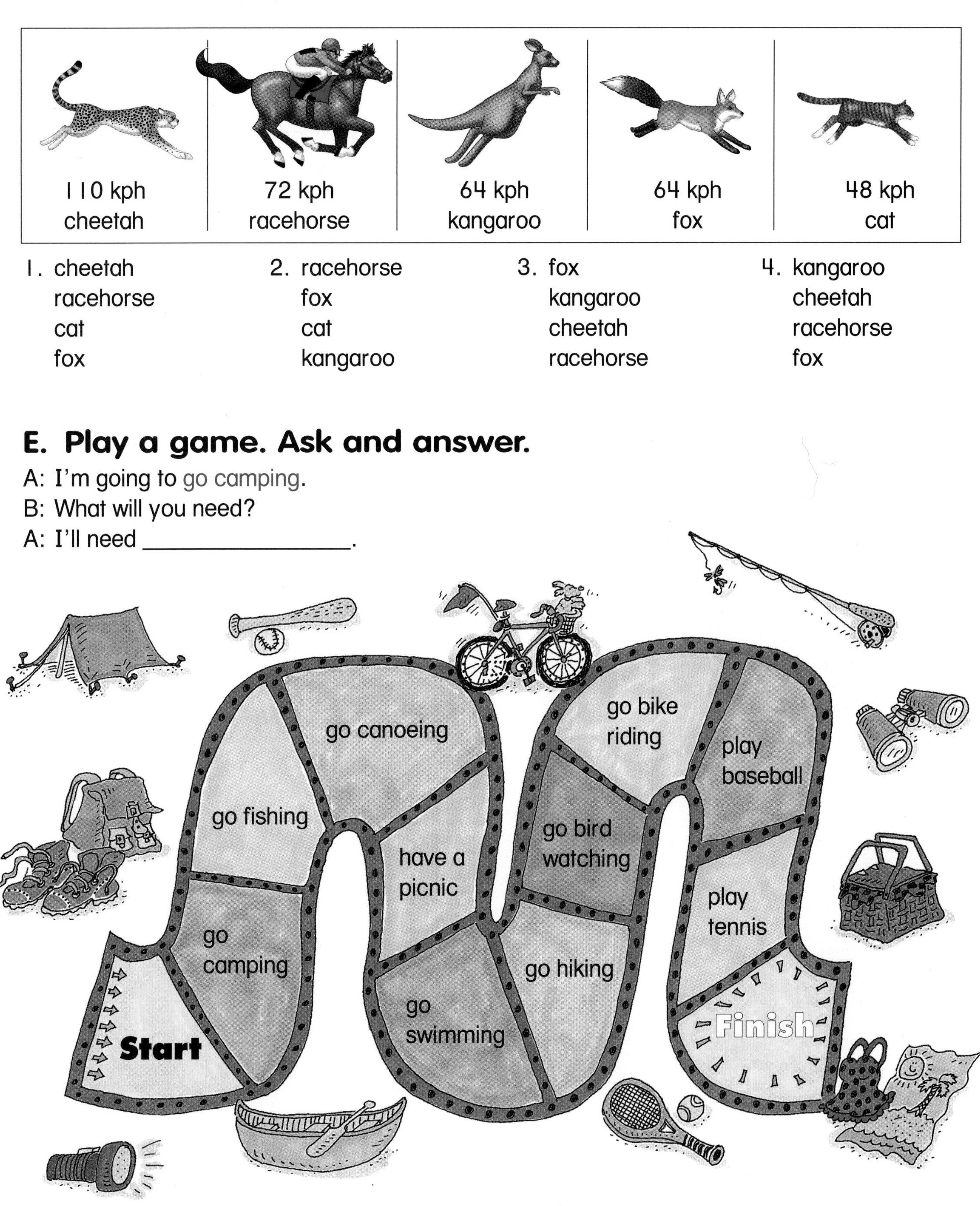

1. cheetah
   racehorse
   cat
   fox
2. racehorse
   fox
   cat
   kangaroo
3. fox
   kangaroo
   cheetah
   racehorse
4. kangaroo
   cheetah
   racehorse
   fox

E. Play a game. Ask and answer.

A: I'm going to go camping.
B: What will you need?
A: I'll need ________________.

Let's Talk

Beth: I hate winter. I'm tired of the cold and snow.
Anna: Not me! Winter is my favorite season.
Beth: Why?
Anna: Because I like skiing.

Anna: Which season do you like best?
Beth: I like summer best because I like swimming.
Anna Oh, look! There's Mark. Let's catch up with him.
Beth: OK.

Anna: Hey, Mark. Wait for us.
Mark: OK, but please hurry up. I'm cold.
Anna: We're walking as fast as we can.

Beth: Oh, no! Not again!

Wait for	us.
	me.
OK.	

Seasons

winter spring summer fall

Ask and answer.

> Why does he like winter best?
> He likes winter best because he likes ice skating.

1. ice skating

2. waterskiing

3. planting flowers

4. jumping into leaves

5. swimming

6. playing football

7. skiing

8. flying kites

What about you?

Which season do you like best? Why?

Let's Learn

Last summer Kevin and his family went to a dude ranch.

Every day Kevin worked outside with the ranch hands and rode a horse.

At night everyone ate dinner around a campfire. Then the ranch hands told stories.

Kevin and his family made a lot of new friends. Next summer they're going to go back there again.

Grammar Focus

past	now	future
yesterday	today	tomorrow
last week	this week	next week
last month	this month	next month
last year	this year	next year

Ask and answer.

What did she do last summer?
She went to a dude ranch.
What's she going to do next summer?
She's going to go to the beach.

1.

last summer

next summer

2.

yesterday

tomorrow

3.

last month

next month

4.

last week

next week

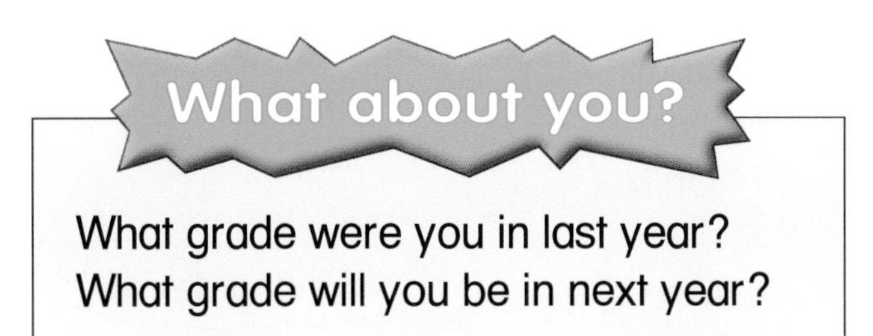

What grade were you in last year?
What grade will you be in next year?

Let's Read

Vincent's Report

I always thought December was the coldest month of the year. But December isn't cold everywhere.

I live in Minnesota in the United States. In December, it's winter here. It's cold and there's a lot of snow and ice. During winter vacation I usually go skiing and ice skating.

December in Minnesota

Last year I went to Australia in December. I was surprised. The weather was hot and sunny. I went swimming and sailing every day.

December in Australia

The seasons are different in the United States and Australia because these two countries are on opposite sides of the world. When it's winter in the United States, it's summer in Australia.

New Words

thought
Minnesota
the United States
ice
Australia
sailing
countries
opposite sides

Answer the questions.

1. Is it hot and sunny in Minnesota in December?
2. What does Vincent usually do during winter vacation?
3. Where is it summer in December?
4. Why are the seasons different in the United States and Australia?

True or false?

1. December is cold everywhere.
2. There is a lot of snow and ice in Minnesota in December.
3. You can go swimming and sailing in December in Australia.
4. The United States and Australia are on the same side of the world.

Choose a title.

Which is the best title for Vincent's report?

a. Skiing
b. Sailing
c. Seasons

Vocabulary

What does "seasons" mean?

a. winter, spring, summer, fall
b. January, February, March
c. Monday, Tuesday, Wednesday

Sounds and Sentences

The squid squeezed into the little square.

The queen answered the question on the quiz.

Let's Chant

Last Summer, What Did You Do?

Last summer, what did you do?
  I went to Hawaii.
I did, too.
Did you buy anything?
  Yes, I did. I bought a two-dollar tie.
So did I.

Last winter, where did you go?
  I went to London.
So did Joe.
Did you buy anything?
  Yes, I did. I bought English tea.
So did he.

Next winter, what are you going to do?
  We're going to go skiing.
We are, too.
Next summer, where are you going to be?
  We're going to stay home.
So are we.

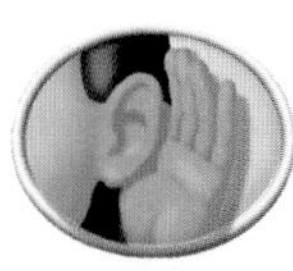

Let's Listen

Listen and check.

1. ☐ Winter is Tim's favorite season.
   ☐ Spring is Tim's favorite season.
2. ☐ Summer is Kim's favorite season.
   ☐ Fall is Kim's favorite season.
3. ☐ Winter is Don's favorite season.
   ☐ Summer is Don's favorite season.
4. ☐ Tess and Lori like fall best.
   ☐ Tess and Lori like spring best.
5. ☐ Pete and Jake like fall best.
   ☐ Pete and Jake like winter best.
6. ☐ Allison likes winter best.
   ☐ Allison likes summer best.

Listen to the answers and check the questions.

1. ☐ What did she do yesterday?
   ☐ What is she going to do tomorrow?

2. ☐ What did he do last month?
   ☐ What is he going to do next month?

3. ☐ What are they going to do next week?
   ☐ What did they do last week?

4. ☐ What is he going to do next summer?
   ☐ What did he do last summer?

5. ☐ What did she do last week?
   ☐ What is she going to do next week?

6. ☐ What are they going to do tomorrow?
   ☐ What did they do yesterday?

Let's Talk

Kevin: I'm hungry! Why don't we make a snack?
Mark: That's a good idea. I'm hungry, too. What do you have to eat?

Kevin: Well, there's some peanut butter and jelly and some bread in the cupboard. And we have some potato chips and bananas, too.
Mark: Great!

Kevin: Is there anything in the refrigerator?
Mark: Let's see. There's some ham and cheese, and there are some pickles.
Kevin: Perfect! Let's use it all.

Why don't we make a snack?
That's a good idea.
No, I don't want to.

Say these.

There **is** some juice.
There **is** some cake.

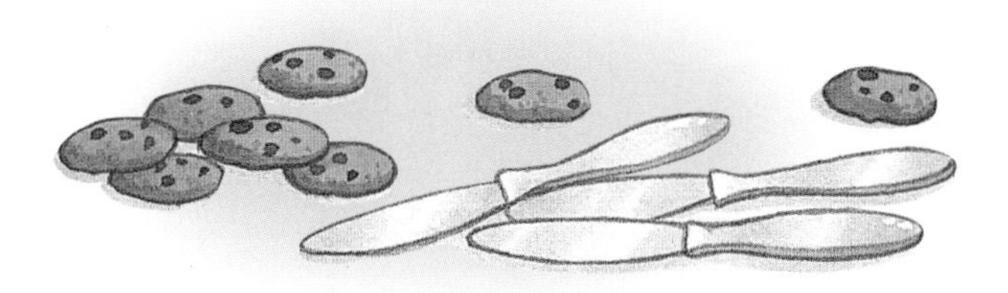

There **are** some cookies.
There **are** some knives.

Ask and answer.

What's in the blue picnic basket?
There is some cake and there are some plates.

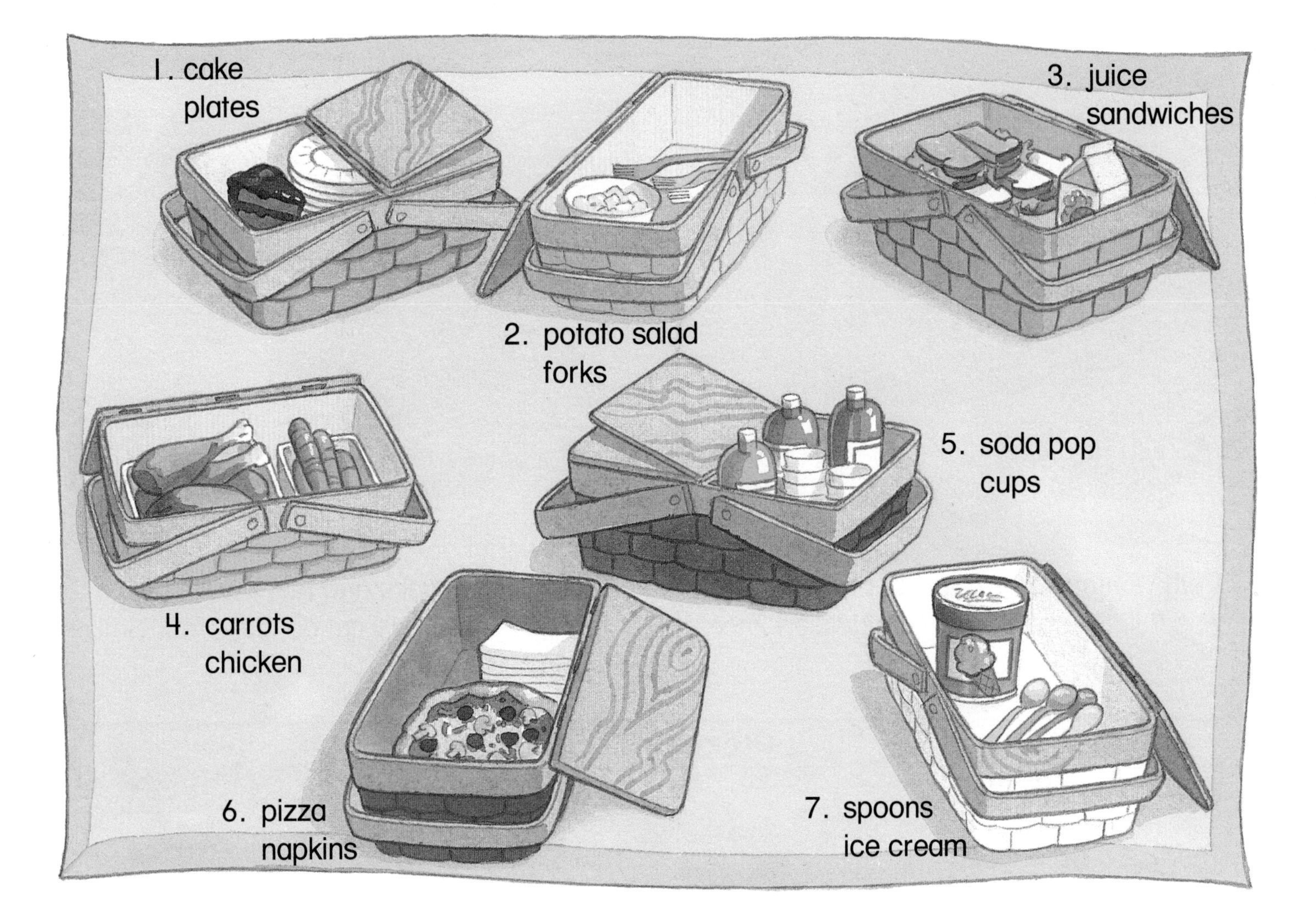

Let's Learn

Last week Beth and her family went to a picnic. Beth was very hungry. She put a lot of food on her plate.

Then she saw the desserts. There were a lot of cookies and there was a big chocolate cake. Everything looked delicious.

Beth wanted some cake, but her plate was full. She decided to get dessert later.

Beth went back to get some dessert, but there was no cake and there were only a few cookies. She was too late. Poor Beth!

Grammar Focus

How much cake is there?

There is **a little** cake.
There is **a lot of** cake.

How many cookies are there?

There are **a lot of** cookies.
There are **a few** cookies.

Ask and answer.

How much water is there?
There is | a little / a lot of | water.

How many oranges are there?
There are | a few / a lot of | oranges.

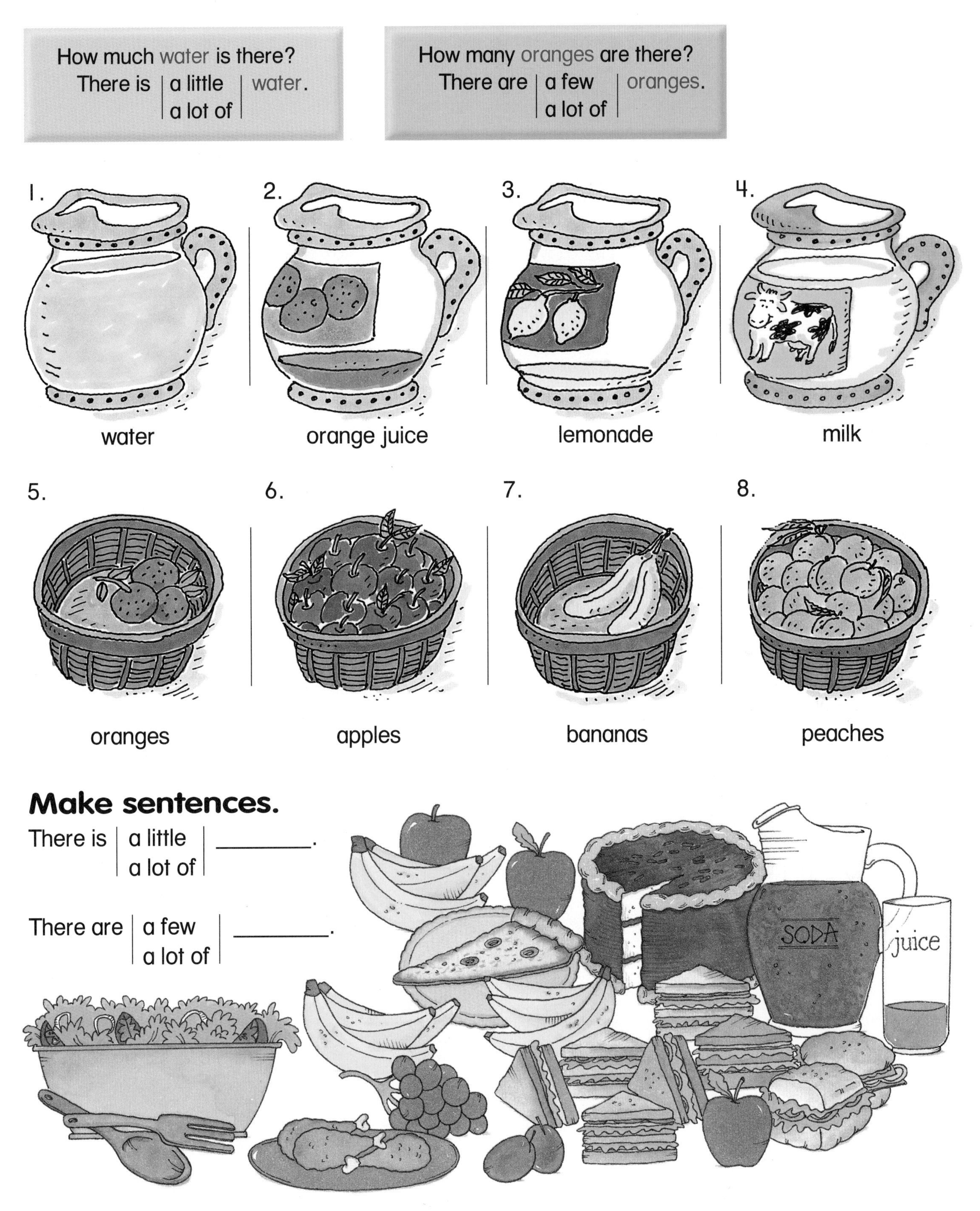

Make sentences.

There is | a little / a lot of | ________.

There are | a few / a lot of | ________.

Let's Read

Rachel's Report

Fat and Sugar
Protein
Fruits
Vegetables
Grains

The Food Pyramid

Do you know how to choose healthy food? The food pyramid can help you. You need to eat a lot of the food at the bottom of the pyramid and only a little of the food at the top.

You need to eat a lot of grains, like rice and bread, every day. You also need to eat a lot of vegetables, like carrots and spinach. Fruits, like apples and oranges, are good for you, too.

You need to eat some protein every day. There is protein in milk, cheese, fish, and eggs. Dessert is delicious, but be careful. You don't need to eat a lot of fat or sugar.

Use the food pyramid every day and you will stay healthy.

New Words

healthy	spinach
pyramid	protein
bottom	fat
top	sugar
vegetables	

Answer the questions.

1. What can help you choose healthy food?
2. Are grains good for you?
3. Which food is a vegetable, a carrot or an orange?
4. Is there protein in eggs?

True or false?

1. You need to eat a lot of the food at the bottom of the pyramid.
2. There is protein in fish.
3. Apples are vegetables.
4. Vegetables and fruits are not good for you.

Choose a title.

Which is the best title for Rachel's report?

a. Food
b. Fruits and Vegetables
c. The Food Pyramid

Vocabulary

What does "healthy" mean?

a. not hungry
b. not good for you
c. good for you

Sounds and Sentences

Let's Chant

How Much Do You Want?

How much do you want?
Not too much.
Just a little.
Not too much.

A little of this
And a little of that.
Just a little.
Not too much.

How many do you want?
Not too many.
Just a few.
One or two.

A few of these
And a few of those.
Just a few.
One or two.

Not too much.
Just a little.
Not too many.
Just a few.

Not too much.
Just a little.
Just a few.
One or two.

Let's Listen

Listen and check.

1. Brett				
2. Kathy				
3. Eric				
4. June				

True or false? Listen and check.

1. ☐ True ☐ False
2. ☐ True ☐ False
3. ☐ True ☐ False
4. ☐ True ☐ False
5. ☐ True ☐ False
6. ☐ True ☐ False
7. ☐ True ☐ False
8. ☐ True ☐ False

Let's Review

A. Fill in the blanks. Then say and act.

1. **Anna:** Winter is my favorite season.
Beth: _____?
Anna: Because __________________.
Which season __________?
Beth: I like summer best because
________________.

2. **Kevin:** I'm hungry. Why don't we
________________?
Mark: That's a good idea. I'm
_______________, too. What
___________?
Kevin: Well, there's some _____________
in the cupboard. And we have
some ________________, too.
Mark: Great!

B. Ask your partner.

How old were you last year?
How old will you be next year?
What did you do last summer?
What will you do next summer?

C. Answer the question.

What's in your refrigerator at home?

D. Listen and circle.

a few apples | a lot of apples

a little potato salad | a lot of potato salad

a little ham | a lot of ham

a few cookies | a lot of cookies

a little milk | a lot of milk

a few eggs | a lot of eggs

E. Play a game. Ask and answer.

A: How many peaches are there?
B: There are | a few / a lot of | peaches.

A: How much cake is there?
B: There is | a little / a lot of | cake.

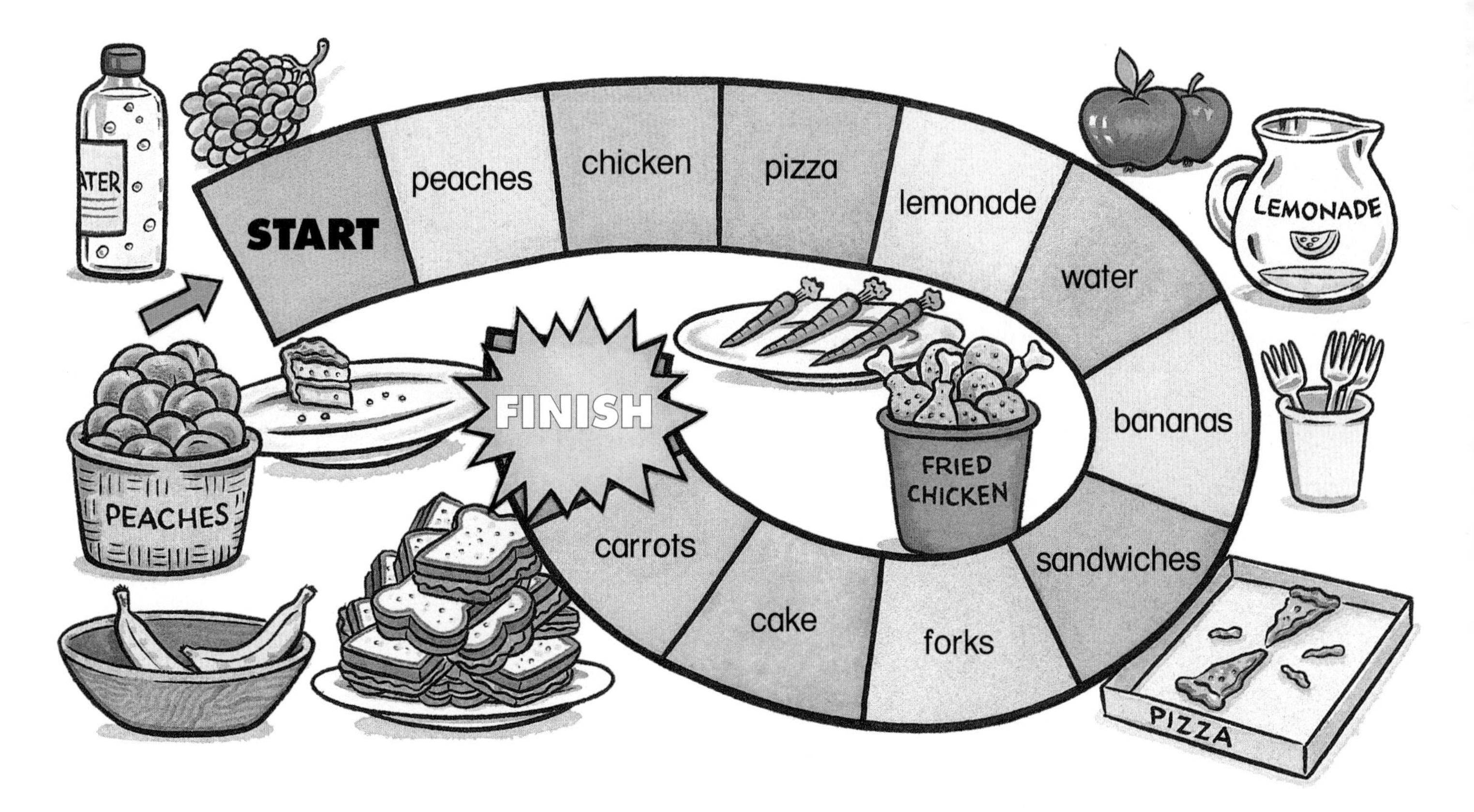

Let's Talk

Anna: Who's that?
Kevin: That was me when I was two years old.
Anna: That's a cute picture.

Anna: What about that picture? Is that you, too?
Kevin: Yeah.
Anna: When did you learn how to ride a bike?
Kevin: Oh, I don't remember. I think I was four years old.
Anna: Did you want to be a firefighter?
Kevin: Yes, I did. That bike was my fire engine.

Kevin: What about you? What did you want to be when you were little?
Anna: I wanted to be a police officer, and a ballerina, and a princess!

What did you want to be when you were little?
I wanted to be a police officer.

Ask and answer.

When did he learn how to ride a bike?
He learned how to ride a bike when he was six.

1. ride a bike
   six

2. play baseball
   seven

3. do a somersault
   five

4. do a cartwheel
   nine

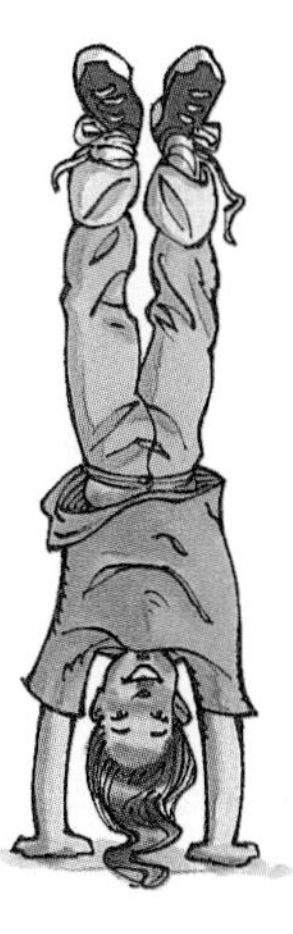

5. do a handstand
   eight

6. write his name
   four

7. swim
   six

8. read
   five

What about you?

When did you learn how to ride a bike?

Let's Learn

When the bell rang this morning, the students were in their seats. It was 8:30, but the teacher wasn't there.

At 8:45, the teacher walked into the classroom. It was very noisy. Some students were studying, but other students were talking and laughing.

When the students saw the teacher, the noise stopped. Everyone became quiet.

Then the teacher heard a funny sound. He looked around the room. Oh, no! Mark was snoring.

Grammar Focus

The students were studying **when the teacher walked into the room.**

When the teacher walked into the room, the students were studying.

Ask and answer.

What was she doing when the doorbell rang?
She was doing her homework when the doorbell rang.

What were you doing when the teacher walked into the classroom today?	**OR**	What was your teacher doing when you walked into the classroom today?

Alice's Report

Last year I went on a homestay to the United States. I lived with the Johnson family in the state of California. When I was there, I went to school with my American sister, Julie.

At first, speaking English every day was hard. I was homesick. But then I started to enjoy my homestay. English was easier. School was fun.

I liked living with the Johnsons. We ate dinner together every night. We went to the movies a lot. During spring vacation, we went on a camping trip.

Now I'm back home with my parents. I often write to my American family and they write to me. Next year the Johnsons are going to visit me.

New Words

homestay	American
state	homesick
California	enjoy

Answer the questions.

1. What did Alice do last year?
2. In her American family, did Alice have any brothers or sisters?
3. What did the Johnsons and Alice do during spring vacation?
4. When will Alice see the Johnson family again?

True or false?

1. Alice went on a homestay to Canada.
2. At first, speaking English was easy for Alice.
3. Alice ate dinner with the Johnsons every night.
4. The Johnsons often write to Alice.

Choose a title.

Which is the best title for Alice's report?

a. Alice's Homestay
b. The Johnson Family
c. Camping in the United States

Vocabulary

What does "homesick" mean?

a. wants to go home
b. stays home
c. feels sick

Sounds and Sentences

Let's Chant

How Old Were You?

How old were you when you learned how to run?
I was one.
I was one.
How old were you when you went to the zoo?
I was two.
I was two.
How old were you when you started to ski?
I was three.
I was three.
How old were you when you helped at the store?
I was four.
I was four.
How old were you when you learned how to dive?
I was five.
I was five.

I was five when I learned how to dive.
I was four when I helped at the store.
I was three when I started to ski.
I was two when I went to the zoo.
I was one when I learned how to run.

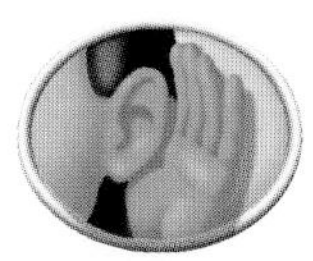

Let's Listen

True or false? Listen and check.

1. ☐ True ☐ False	2. ☐ True ☐ False	3. ☐ True ☐ False	4. ☐ True ☐ False	5. ☐ True ☐ False	6. ☐ True ☐ False

Listen and write the letter.

____ 1. Bill learned how to do a somersault
____ 2. Jenny learned how to ride a bike
____ 3. When Robin was eight
____ 4. When Andy was nine
____ 5. Barb learned how to do a cartwheel
____ 6. When Dale was five

a. when she was six.
b. when she was seven.
c. he learned how to play baseball.
d. he learned how to write his name.
e. she learned how to do a handstand.
f. when he was four.

Let's Talk

Beth: Anna, look!
Anna: What is it?
Beth: It's an airplane ticket. I'm going to France this summer!
Anna: Wow! When are you going?
Beth: In July. I'll be there for three weeks.

Anna: Have you ever been to France?
Beth: No, I haven't. I've never been out of the country.
Anna: Me neither. Who are you going with?
Beth: I'm going with my aunt. I'm so excited!

Anna: Oh, Beth, you're so lucky!
Beth: Yes, but there's one problem.
Anna: What?
Beth: I can't speak French.

I've never been out of the country.
Me neither.

I have = I've

Ask and answer.

Have you ever | eaten burritos?
 | seen a penguin?

Yes, I have.
No, I haven't.

eat → eaten
see → seen
be → been

I've been to ________, but I've never been to ________.
I've eaten ________, but I've never eaten ________.
I've seen ________, but I've never seen ________.

Let's Learn

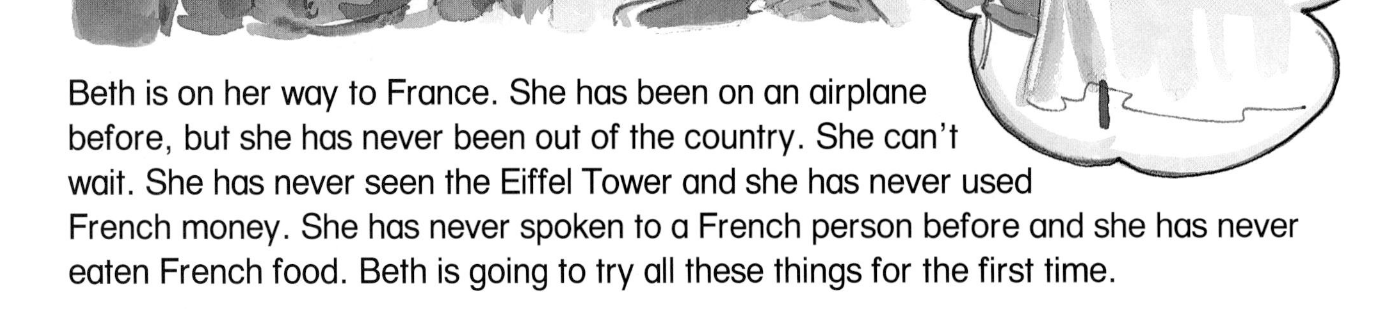

Beth is on her way to France. She has been on an airplane before, but she has never been out of the country. She can't wait. She has never seen the Eiffel Tower and she has never used French money. She has never spoken to a French person before and she has never eaten French food. Beth is going to try all these things for the first time.

Grammar Focus

bake →	have baked	go →	have gone	speak →	have spoken
be →	have been	read →	have read	stay up →	have stayed up
drive →	have driven	ride →	have ridden	use →	have used
eat →	have eaten	see →	have seen	watch →	have watched
fly →	have flown	sleep →	have slept	write →	have written

Play a game. Ask and answer.

Have you ever been to New York?
Yes, I have.
No, I haven't.

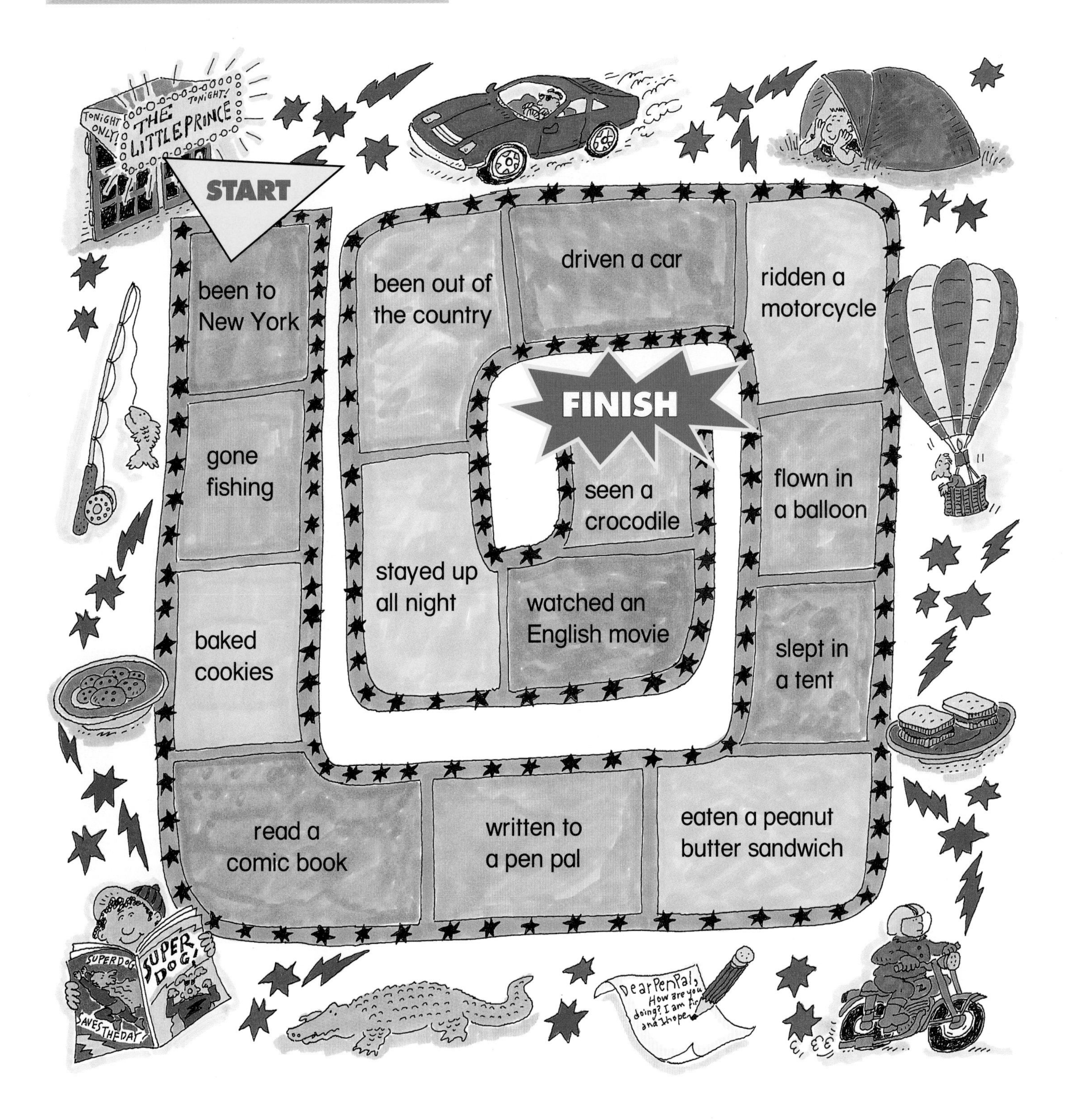

Beth's Report

Have you ever been to Paris? I was there this summer. It is a great place to visit! Here are some fun things to do in Paris.

Eat breakfast outside at a sidewalk cafe. French pastries are delicious.

Go for a walk along the Seine River. You can see many artists painting and selling their pictures. You can buy books and postcards, too.

Ride the subway to the Eiffel Tower. The view from the top is fantastic!

Just remember one thing. Learn some French words before you go. Then you can speak French in Paris!

New Words

Paris	Seine River
place	subway
sidewalk cafe	Eiffel Tower
pastries	view
along	fantastic

Answer the questions.

1. Are there fun things to do in Paris?
2. Where can you eat breakfast in Paris?
3. What can you buy along the Seine River?
4. Can you go to the top of the Eiffel Tower?

True or false?

1. There aren't any sidewalk cafes in Paris.
2. The subway goes to the Eiffel Tower.
3. You can see many artists painting and selling their pictures by the Seine River.
4. People in Paris speak French.

Choose a title.

Which is the best title for Beth's report?

a. Great Places to Visit
b. Visiting Paris
c. The Eiffel Tower

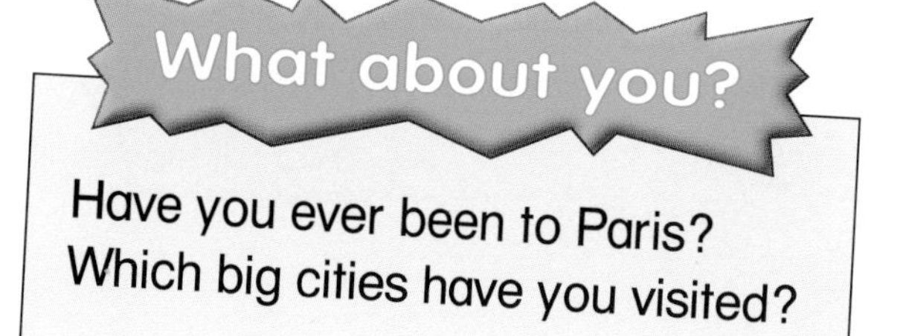

Vocabulary

What does "sidewalk cafe" mean?

a. a restaurant with tables inside
b. a restaurant with tables outside
c. a restaurant inside a store

Sounds and Sentences

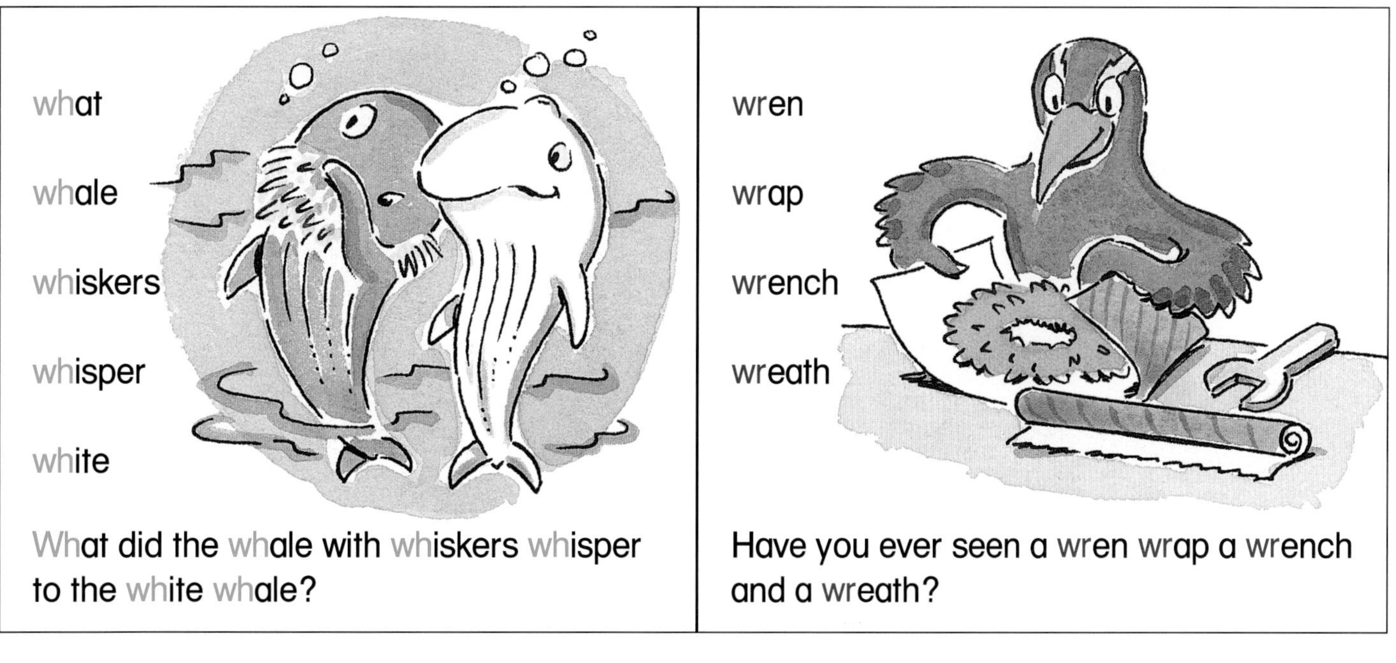

Let's Sing

Have You Ever Broken Your Elbow?

Have you ever broken your elbow?
Have you ever eaten a snail?
Have you ever ridden a rhino?
Or stepped on a lion's tail?

No, I've never broken my elbow.
I've never eaten a snail.
I've never ridden a rhino.
Or stepped on a lion's tail.

Have you ever driven a taxi?
Have you ever flown your own plane?
Have you ever forgotten your book bag
On a bus in the middle of Spain?

No, I've never driven a taxi.
I've never flown my own plane.
But one day I forgot my beautiful book bag
On a bus in the middle of Spain.

Let's Listen

Listen and check.

✔ = yes ✘ = no

	burrito	penguin	France	llama	sushi	England
Kelly	✔	✔	✘	✔	✔	✘
Drew	✘	✘	✔	✘	✔	✔

1. ☐ Yes, he has.
   ☐ No, he hasn't.
2. ☐ Yes, she has.
   ☐ No, she hasn't.
3. ☐ Yes, he has.
   ☐ No, he hasn't.
4. ☐ Yes, she has.
   ☐ No, she hasn't.

Listen and fill in the chart.

✔ = yes ✘ = no

	slept in a tent	seen a crocodile	gone fishing	been to New York	flown in a balloon	ridden a motorcycle
Rob						
Lori						
Adam						
Kristy						
Debbie						
Paul						

Let's Review

A. Fill in the blanks. Then say and act.

1. **Anna:** Did you want ____________ when you were little?
   Kevin: Yes, ________. That bike was my fire engine. What about you? ________________ when you were little?
   Anna: I ____________________.

2. **Anna:** Have you ever ________ France?
   Beth: No, ________. I've never been out of the country.
   Anna: Me neither. Who ____________?
   Beth: I'm going with ____________. I'm so excited!

B. Ask your partner.

When did you learn how to ride a bike?
When did you learn how to do a somersault?
When did you learn how to write your name?
When did you learn how to read?

C. Answer the question.

Have you ever been out of the country?
Where did you go?

D. Listen and number the pictures.

What were the children doing when it started to rain?

E. Ask your friends.

Have you ever ____________?

Names	me					
ridden a horse						
flown in an airplane						
gone camping						
seen a kangaroo						
been to Australia						
eaten potato salad						

Let's Go 5 Syllabus

UNIT	LANGUAGE ITEMS	FUNCTIONS	TOPICS
1	I'm (Beth). I'm (12). I'm (10) years old. My name's (Mark). My best friend is (Anna). What's (her) name? (Her) name is (Beth). How old is (she)? (She's) (10) years old. Does (she) have any brothers or sisters? (She) has (two brothers). (She) doesn't have any brothers or sisters. What does (she) like to do? (She) likes to (play computer games). What does (she) want to be? (She) wants to be (an engineer). What's (he) going to do? (He's) going to (play soccer). What does (he) have to do? (He) has to (wash the dishes). What does (he) want to do? (He) wants to (sail a boat). Why did (she) stay home yesterday? (She) stayed home because (she had a stomachache). Which one is (bigger)? The (dog) is (bigger).	Self-identification Asking about and expressing one's age Describing who people are Asking about and describing what someone wants to be Asking about and describing what someone likes to do	Introductions Family Comparisons Activities Occupations
2	Have a good trip. Thanks. See you Monday. What does (he) look like? (He) has (red hair) and (green eyes). Which (girl) is (Brian's cousin)? (His cousin) is the (girl) with (curly red hair)./(His cousin) is the (girl) in the (blue pants and striped shirt).	Wishing someone a good time Describing people's hair color and style Describing people's eye color Identifying people by their clothing and features	Family Physical appearance
3	Would you like to (go camping) with us? Sure! I'd love to. Thanks, but I can't. (He's) going to (go camping) tomorrow. What will (he) need? (He'll) need (a tent) and (a flashlight). It'll be (hot) tomorrow. I'll need (a jacket). I won't need (a jacket). What will (they) do tomorrow? (They'll) (go canoeing).	Extending, accepting, and declining invitations Talking about the future using *will* Asking about and expressing needs Describing tomorrow's temperature	Outdoor activities and equipment Temperature

UNIT	LANGUAGE ITEMS	FUNCTIONS	TOPICS
4	What do you think? I think (geography) is (easy). I think (geography) is (easier) than (math). Which subject is (easier), (geography) or (science)? Which one is the (fastest)? The (cheetah) is the (fastest). The (fox) is as (fast) as the (kangaroo).	Eliciting and expressing personal opinion Comparing school subjects Comparing animal sizes and speeds	School subjects Animals
5	Wait for (us). OK. Why does (he) like (winter) best? (He) likes (winter) best because (he) likes (ice skating). What did (she) do (last summer)? (She) went (to a dude ranch). What's (she) going to do (next summer)? (She's) going to go (to the beach).	Requesting that someone wait Asking about and expressing personal preference Asking about and stating what someone did Asking about and stating what someone is going to do	Seasons Seasonal activities
6	Why don't we (make a snack)? That's a good idea. No, I don't want to. There is some (juice). There are some (cookies). How much (water) is there? There is a little (water). There is a lot of (water). How many (oranges) are there? There are a few (oranges). There are a lot of (oranges).	Making, agreeing with, and declining suggestions Asking about and stating quantities	Countable and uncountable food items
7	What did you want to be when you were little? I wanted to be (a police officer). When did (he) learn how to (ride a bike)? (He) learned how to (ride a bike) when (he) was (six). What was (she) doing when (the doorbell rang)? (She) was (doing her homework) when (the doorbell rang). When (the doorbell rang), (she) was (doing her homework).	Talking about childhood hopes and dreams Asking and stating when someone learned to do something Asking and stating what someone was doing when something else happened	Childhood hopes and dreams Childhood milestones
8	I've never been out of the country. Me neither. Have you ever (been to Paris)? Yes, I have. No, I haven't. I've (seen a penguin) but I've never (seen a cheetah).	Asking about and talking about experiences	New and prior experiences Travel

Word List

T

U

V

W

Y

Z